Sortie Not

Our search for a lost bomber crew

A & R Armstrong

First published in 2003 by

P3 Publications

13 Beaver Road, Carlisle CA2 7PS

British Library Cataloguing in Publication Data
A catalogue record for this book is available from the British Library
ISBN 09537203 7 3

Recommended price £3.99

1

CONTENTS

Printed in the UK by:
Ink Truck
Lorne Crescent
Carlisle
CA2 5XW

INTRODUCTION

The 207 Squadron bomber crew whose short history is traced in this story failed to complete their sixth operational flight on the night of 24/25 July 1944.

THEIR SORTIE WAS NOT COMPLETED

Our research into these young men has been quite difficult. All we had at the outset was a letter sent to my late mother over fifty years ago, a copy of which is printed overleaf, and the knowledge that it referred to a young man called Ross who had been killed in an aircraft during the war.

From these very unpromising beginnings we have managed to slowly piece together not only his story but also that of those who served with him.

Unlike the aircrew, our sortie is completed and the story of everything we have found can be read on the following pages.

This work is dedicated to the men and women of Bomber Command 1939 - 1945.

NOT FORGOTTEN

Errol.
43, Heather Road.
Newport, Mon.
26th. Aug. 44.

Dear Miss Hall,

Ross's mother and dad were very pleased to receive your letter, they will be answering it soon.

As Ross's aunt I feel I would like to write you. Ross has often spoken about you and your family to his mum and dad who were most grateful for the way in which you received him.

Ross was loved and admired by all who knew him, and his parents idolised him, and had planned such a grand career for him, so you can imagine the strain they are under in the anxious days that lie ahead.

They are to be admired for the brave way in which they are carrying their heavy burden.

I am staying a few weeks with my sister and brother-in-law, whom I felt need a bit of companionship, although I am afraid, there is so very little one can do or say, that will make things easier for them.

I am sorry to say that no further word has been received about Ross, but you can rest assured that as soon as they hear anything, you will get to know.

My sister had a letter from David's mum who informed her that David's body had been found, and that he was buried in London fortnight yesterday. His mother has returned

to Liverpool for a short stay, so I am hoping to visit her when I return to Liverpool. Ross's parents would like to meet you, your family sometime, so in the meantime I hope that you will continue to correspond with them, and also myself.

Yours very sincerely
Mary Rigby (Mrs.)

The letter that began it all.

A transcription is given on the opposite page

4

Errol,
43 Heather Road,
Newport, Mon.
26 Aug 44.

Dear Miss Hall,

Ross's mother and dad were pleased to receive your letter, they will be answering it soon.

As Ross's aunt I feel I would like to write you. Ross had often spoken about you and your family to his mum and dad who were most grateful for the way in which you received him.

Ross was loved and admired by all who knew him and his parents idolized him, and had planned such a grand career for him, so you can imagine the strain they are under in the arduous days that lie ahead. They are to be admired for the brave way in which they are carrying this heavy burden.

I am staying a few weeks with my sister and brother in law, who I feel need a bit of companionship, although I am afraid, there is so very little one can do or say, that will make things easier for them. I am sorry to say that no further word has been received about Ross, but you can rest assured that as soon as they hear anything, you will get to know.

My sister had a letter from Dave's mum who informed her that Dave's body had been found, and that he was buried in London fortnight yesterday. His mother has returned to Liverpool for a short stay, so I am hoping to visit her when I return to Liverpool. Ross's parents would like to meet you and your family sometime, so in the meantime I hope that you will continue to correspond with them and also myself.

Yours very sincerely,
Mary Rigby (Mrs.)

CHAPTER 1: THE BEGINNING

This brief story began in late 1942 or early 1943, I'm not really sure which, when a rather shy boy from Newport Monmouthshire found himself in Lincolnshire having been called upon to start his training as a bomb aimer in the Royal Air Force Volunteer Reserve. In all probability he had already spent some time in London, first at Euston House, where he'd have undergone aptitude and medical tests for the Pilot, Navigator, Bomb Aimer courses. These completed, he would have moved on to the Aircrew Reception Centre at Lords cricket ground where he would have been for about three weeks before being posted to an Initial Training Wing. In the case of the young man in question he was posted to the I.T.W. at Skegness and then moved on to Boston with other course members, about 30 in all, due to overcrowding at the main site. On arrival in Boston he received some rudimentary kit and along with two other raw recruits was told he was to be billeted with the Hall family who lived at 10 Browns Road in the town. It must have been a happy home and obviously left an impression in his mind, as for the remainder of his short life, he kept in touch with the family who lived there.

This family was made up of father Albert, a brick layer and staunch union official, Annie his wife, a full time housewife who had been orphaned before she was 10 and then served a seven year apprenticeship as a cigar maker before meeting and eventually marrying Albert in 1912. By the time of this story their eldest daughter, Kathleen, was already married and living in Stamford, but their two younger girls, Vinnie (Lavinia) and Frances were still at home with their parents, although Vinnie was engaged to a previous R.A.F. 'lodger,' Ken Bonner of Maidstone, Kent, and would marry him in October 1943. At the time of writing they are still together and will celebrate their diamond wedding anniversary in just over a years time. Fran, the baby, was then about 17 and working in an insurance office in the town after leaving the High School at 16. This then was the family that George Ross Shannon came to know well over the ensuing weeks.

Ross, as he preferred to be called, had been born in Walton, Liverpool, on the 6 March 1923. His father, John Dennis Shannon had been born and raised in Barrow in Furness and followed his father into the position of a Customs and Excise Officer. At some time he had moved to Liverpool, a move presumably connected to his profession. Time passed and John Dennis met and married Helen Ross Davidson and then settled at 11 Utting Avenue. Ross was their only child. At some time the family moved again, this time to Newport, another coastal town where John Dennis would continue his work. They settled into a new home in a comfortable area of the town, their address being "Errol," 43 Heather Drive, Newport, and it would have been from here that Ross first enlisted in the Volunteer Reserve and then left later to 'do his bit' for King and Country.

Vin, my aunt who is now aged 83, remembers Ross as rather a quiet shy young man, who had lots of 'nice things'. He was a stickler for order and neatness and was polite and well mannered. Annie, my grandmother, obviously took a shine to him and his colleagues and started to 'mother' them. The lads were sent to their billets with straw mattresses but they were never to sleep on these at Browns Road, instead beds were found and they had their own room. Their washing and ironing was done for them and their sugar ration was increased when Albert insisted his daughters gave up their allocation for the sake of the boys, but Vin recalls that her father didn't see the need to give up his!

Sergeant Mills who was one of the instructors in charge of basic training in Boston eventually knocked on the door and told Annie she was being too soft on her boys. He explained to her that part of the training was to toughen up these young men and it was his belief she wasn't letting this happen. Would she please be less of a mother. She agreed, admitted she was being a little soft on them and said she'd toughen up in her attitude. She closed the door and carried on exactly as before but did it in a more covert way.

Vin is still full of stories about the 'goings on' in Boston in those days. Apparently the families acting as hosts were paid just over £1 per week to feed each of the young men. It was never enough and often everyone had to suffer. On the plus side Vin was working in a shop at the time and she did say that her employer would occasionally help the family out. She also recalls returning home on one occasion to find the living room littered with rather sick looking boys. She enquired as to what was going on and it became clear when she was told they'd all just returned from having 'arm fulls' of inoculations to protect them against every disease known to man. Several veterans have suggested this could well point to their future training being based in Africa rather than North America.

During his stay with the family, a friendship developed between Ross and Frances. How serious this was I have no idea, but I do know that Frances, my mother, never forgot Ross and that I very nearly ended up being given the same Christian name. I know that they kept in touch right up to the end, in fact beyond it, and it was as a direct result of this that our story came about.

Above: Annie and Albert Hall
            (circa 1915)
         with daughter Kathleen

Right: Frances Armstrong
            (nee Hall)
          9/02/26 - 6/05/74

CHAPTER 2: THE ROAD TO 207

We have little knowledge or specific detail of where the crew trained or how they came together. In the future it will be possible to find all this out but not until their personal records come into the public domain in around the year 2017. It seems a long time to wait, but the ruling is that 75 years must pass between enlistment and records being released so there's little that can be done.

A lot of work has gone into finding details of individual crew members and we have slowly managed to piece together quite a lot of their background, which is outlined below. The research has been complex in the extreme and much of it has been carried out by a friend, David Brown. We are most grateful for the time and effort he has invested in this and feel that the information he has uncovered has made our story much more complete.

The Crew

Pilot PETER CAMERON McINTOSH. (171930) R.A.F.V.R.

He was born on the 8.11.1923 at 37 Court Lane, Dulwich, and was the youngest crew member. His father was Orla Calkins McIntosh and his mother Hilda Bessie McIntosh; whose maiden name was Mitchell. In 1923 his father's profession was a mechanical engineer, but at the time of his death he is described as an advertising representative.

From what we can discover 'Mac' did not have a very easy life, his family had at some time moved to 16 Thurleigh Road, Battersea and on 21.3.1940 his mother had died from breast cancer at St. James' Hospital. This was bad enough for a 16 year old to endure, but to then lose his father on 8.6.1940 to tuberculosis, he died at Colindale Hospital Hendon, must represent little less than a tragedy.
What happened to 'Mac' after losing his parents isn't known but whatever it was it couldn't have been long before he enlisted and started his training as a pilot.

He himself was dead before he was 21 and he is buried in Scartho Road Cemetery, Grimsby (Section 116, Row M, Grave 13), the inscription reads thus:

'In loving memory of our dear and only brother. Until we meet again.' From this it would seem safe to assume he had at least two siblings who were responsible for the epitaph. One of these, a sister, was M. H. McIntosh who in 1940 was living at 'Rathcoole,' Ferndale Road, London SW4. We have found that a Mary Hilda McIntosh, born between October and December 1922 did marry Curtis Henwood in the early months of 1945 at Battersea but can trace her no further, it's supposition, but her husband's name hints that he could have been an American and therefore she may have left the country. At the time of writing we have no further information about his family.

Mr. Sid Hiddleston, a fellow pilot and contemporary of McIntosh's on the squadron describes him as follows:

'Small and slight with blonde hair, a great lad who had a bit of a defiant attitude towards authority, he even took the wire out of his cap to make it look floppy and worn.'

At the time of his death his flying hours are given as follows: 165 solo: 36 on type: 78 night solo: 20 night on type and 44 on Inst link. This last entry refers to a ground based apparatus, an early type of flight simulator. He was not very experienced.

On arrival on the squadron he was a Pilot Officer, but received promotion to Flying Officer some time around the end of June/early July 1944.

Flying Officer P.C. McIntosh's Grave; Scartho Road, Cemetery, Grimsby.

Flight Engineer JOSEPH ROBERT GRINT (946690) R.A.F.V.R

Born in Ashington, Northumberland in June 1920. He was the son of Isaac and Jane Ann Grint, maiden name McKenzie.

He was the second eldest of four brothers, the other three being Herbert, Charles George and Isaac.

Prior to serving in the R.A.F.V.R. he had worked at 'Thompsons' a large food store and had also been a successful boxer. His father, Isaac senior, was killed in the colliery on the 7 October 1923, aged 33.

Later his mother remarried and became Mrs. Bruce. We do know he did some of his flight engineer training at Woodford and while there met a young lady called Alma Dickinson. This came about when he was billeted with her aunt in Poynton, and they became good friends.

After he died Alma lost touch with his family until 1946, when, following a visit to his mother, she fell in love with and married Isaac, the youngest of the brothers. Mrs. Grint, now aged 83, and her son Dr. A Grint, have kindly provided us with the above background information. The memory of Joseph Robert Grint is perpetuated on a plaque in a building which is now the Lynemouth Institute.

As an aside, my Aunt distinctly remembers one of the 'lads' being known colloquially as 'Punch'. Could this be a link with Joe Grint's boxing background?

At the time of his death his rank is given as Sergeant. His body was never recovered and he is commemorated at the Air Force Memorial Runnymede, Surrey on panel 230.

Navigator STANLEY WILLIAM GEORGE LITTLE (1450191) R.A.F.V.R.

Born in East Allington, Kingsbridge Devon on 9 June 1923, the son of Walter Stanley and Lillian Jane Little who at the time of their son's death were living in New Malden Surrey, where his father was working as a stationer's salesman. His mother's maiden name was Simpson.

Flight Sergeant Little is buried in Cambridge City Cemetery (grave 13504) on the Air Force Plot for casualties who were stationed in Eastern England. The inscription on the base of his headstone reads:

> 'God's Greatest Gift
> Remembrance
> Mum and Dad.'

Air Bomber   GEORGE ROSS SHANNON (1607839) R.A.F.V.R.

Details of this crew member are given in the previous chapter. At the time of his death his rank was Flight Sergeant, like Sergeant Grint his body was never found and he is commemorated at Runnymede on Panel 222.

Wireless Operator JAMES BEECH (658022) R.A.F.

He was born on the 7.5.1922 at Foxlowe, Market Place, Leek, Staffordshire.

His father was James Beech, a silk weaver, and his mother was Lillian Annie Beech (nee Ratcliffe). At a later date James Senior had himself joined the R.A.F. and at the time of his son's death was serving in Canada.

James Junior had initially joined the Army and had been involved in the landings that took place in Norway. These were at Namsos and Aandalsnes in the spring of 1940. They were ultimately unsuccessful and troops were withdrawn as the Germans advanced.

At some stage, when or why we do not know, James Junior transferred from the Army to the R.A.F. and was eventually posted to Bomber Command.

He was the only married crew member, his wife being Hilda Victoria Beech from the Linton area of Cambridgeshire, who he married on August 25 1941. We cannot find any record of them having children but we do know that his widow later remarried.

His body was also never found and again he is commemorated at Runnymede on Panel 224.

Sergeant Beech is the only crew member listed as Royal Air Force rather than Royal Air Force Volunteer Reserve.

Mid upper gunner LAURENCE DAVID BATEMAN (1447334) R.A.F.V.R.

Dave, as he's referred to in the letter sent to my mother on the 26 August 1944, was born on 23.7.1921 at 47 London Road, Barnsbury, Islington London. He was the son of John Joseph and Ellen Bateman who were living in Kings Cross London when he died. His mother's maiden name was Fruin. His father was an ostler contractor.

Sergeant Bateman was buried on 11 August 1944 at Islington Cemetery, Section P, Joint Grave 23550 (Screen Wall Panel).

It would seem likely that Dave and Ross were 'pals' and that there is a connection to the Liverpool area. The following quotation from the letter sent to my mother would seem to support this:

'My sister (Mrs. Shannon, mother of Ross) had a letter from Dave's mum who informed her that Dave's body had been found, and that he was buried in London a fortnight yesterday. His mother has returned

to Liverpool for a short stay so I am hoping to visit her when I return to Liverpool.
'Mary Rigby 26/8/44
(Maternal Aunt of G.R.Shannon)

It's obvious from the above that addresses were known and that the families knew each other well enough to visit.

Rear gunner ARTHUR WILLIAM SMITH (1338175) R.A.F.V.R.

Flight Sergeant Smith was posted from 619 Squadron, based at Dunholme Lodge, sometime between the 12 and 24 July. He had originally joined the above Squadron on 26.2 1944 from 51 base when the Squadron was stationed at Coningsby. His crew was as follows:

P/O G.G. Runnalls	Pilot
F/Sgt. E.G.I. Matthews	Navigator
Sgt. D.L. Smithson	Bomb Aimer
Sgt. F.E. Butler	Wireless Operator
Sgt. A.W. Smith	Mid Upper Gunner
Sgt. R.G. Simmons	Rear Gunner

No Flight Engineer is given.
This crew had spent some of their time training at 14 O.T.U. based at Husbands Bosworth. On 16.9.1943 they took off at 10.08 in Wellington 1C L7897 and at 10.32 a cylinder head blew off one of the engines. This large piece of metal penetrated the side of the fuselage and nearly hit the navigator. Runnalls was unable to maintain height and made a forced landing two miles south of the airfield. The crew evacuated quickly and avoided the ensuing fire.

As far as can be established Sgt. Smith flew his first sortie on 1.3.44 with a crew captained by P/O L. Warner R.A.A.F. this was to Stuttgart.

He does not appear to have flown again until the 11 April when he flew to Aachen with P/O A. Whiteley and crew.

On the 17 April 619 Squadron transferred to Dunholme Lodge and on the 20 Sgt. Smith again flew with P/O Whiteley on an attack to La Chapelle. He was eventually reunited with his original crew on 3.5.44 when P/O Runnalls took them to attack Mailly-le-Camp. By now the Navigator of this crew was Sgt. A.C.G. Bell and the Flight Engineer was Sgt. J.P. Heather-Hayes.

He carried on a successful association with this crew for a further seven sorties attacking the following targets:

Salbris 7.5.44,	Gennevilliers 9.5.44,
Bourg Leopold 11.5.44,	Amiens 19.5.44,
Duisburg 21.5.44,	Brunswick 22.5.44,
Wesseling 21.6.44.	

Finally he flew one raid, his second with P/O Warner to Marquis Mimoyecques on 27 June before his transfer to 207 Squadron.

At some point he was promoted to Flight Sergeant and he was on his first sortie with the McIntosh crew when he was killed. His body was never recovered and he is also commemorated at the Runnymede Memorial on panel 222.

His background on active service seems unusual. As can be seen above he arrived on 619 with an established crew at the end of February but did not fly with them until early May. He also had a period of almost 6 weeks, from early March to mid April when he appears to have been non-operational.

Reasons for this are unknown, all we can say is that the Runnalls crew are missing from 619 operational records for a considerable time. They then went through a busy spell, before Smith was posted to 207 Squadron. He died on his thirteenth sortie.

During their time at 207 Squadron the crew had links with the following airmen:

Gunner SERGEANT W.R. BURTON (R219660) R.C.A.F.

Sergeant Burton flew as rear gunner with the McIntosh crew on three operational sorties. He was seriously wounded on the St. Leu D'esserent attack during the early hours of the 5 July and never flew with them again. He arrived on 207 Squadron from 51 Base on 24 June (Form 540 page 285) and was a member of the R.C.A.F. We do know that he subsequently lost the sight of one eye as the result of his injuries so can only assume that his flying career was over. No other details are known.

Gunner SERGEANT T.J. DAWSON or DOWSON

Sergeant Dawson joined the crew on their fourth operation to Caen. Nothing is known about him.

Gunner HUGH GRAHAM HAMILTON (1568684) R.A.F.V.R.

This gunner flew with the crew on the 18/19 July on the sortie to Revigny, their fifth operation. He never flew with them again. His rank was Sergeant. He arrived on the Squadron from 51 Base on the 9 July. He was subsequently killed in action on 26 August 1944 when acting as mid upper gunner in the crew of F/L Harding. The aircraft flown was Lancaster 1 PD 216 EM-J and the target was Darmstadt. All were lost and are now buried in Durnbach War Cemetery.

Flight Engineer BRIGGS

Sergeant Briggs replaced Grint as Flight Engineer for the attack to Revigny. Grint had been injured on the third op. but was fit to fly the fourth. He then gave way to Briggs on the fifth and returned himself for the sixth and final flight. Why this came about is not clear and nothing else is known about the subsequent career of Sergeant Briggs.

Gunner G.E. BARKER

Flight Sergeant Barker replaced Bateman on the attack to St. Leu D'esserent. It was the only operation he flew with the crew. No other information is known about him.

Training

Without access to service records it has proved impossible to follow the individual paths taken through training by the young men involved in this story. Bearing this is mind the best course of action appears to be a general overview of aircrew preparation, interspersed with more detailed sections covering the areas of the training programme where we have managed to track our crew down.

We do know they had all volunteered for aircrew duty as this was allied forces policy during the war. We can also be certain that some of the crew, the pilot, navigator and bomb aimer at least, would have spent several months abroad honing their skills as part of the 'Empire Air Training Scheme'. This work took place in many countries including Canada, U.S.A., South Africa and Rhodesia but where they were sent we do not know. The only other certainty we have about early training is that JR. Grint was stationed for a time at Woodford near Manchester where a Flight Engineers School was in operation. Where the gunners and wireless operator trained we are unsure, but it seems likely that Sgt. Beech was stationed in the Linton area earlier in the war, where he met and married his future wife.

On returning to the United Kingdom the pilot, navigator and bomb aimer would have attended an Advanced Flying Unit (A.F.U.) though probably not the same one. They would then have moved on to an Operational Training Unit (O.T.U.) where the basis of a crew was formed. This 'crewing up' was done on a very informal basis when men of all aircrew roles were 'herded' into a hangar and told to sort themselves out as best they could. It was this rather haphazard process which formed the groups of men whose future survival may very well depend on how they eventually 'gelled' as a bomber crew.

At this stage the embryonic team would have consisted of 6 men, later to be joined by the flight engineer. Time spent at the O.T.U., many of which were scattered throughout Britain was relatively short and after three months, often spent flying twin engined 'Wellington' aircraft, crews moved on to the next phase of their training.

In the case of the McIntosh crew this would have been a Heavy Conversion Unit (H.C.U.) where they would have teamed up with the last piece of the jigsaw mentioned above and been intensively schooled in flying four engined aircraft.

This would have taken place at one of the following: R.A.F. Swinderby which is situated on the eastern side of the A46, 8 miles from Lincoln and 7 from Newark (1660 H.C.U. codes TV and YW), this airfield seems the most likely site of our crew's Heavy Conversion Training. Since May 1942 it had been home to crews headed for 5 Group operational squadrons, and had become so crowded by 1944 that over 3000 aircrew were stationed there undergoing conversion courses. At one stage during that year there was the need to install double bunks in the already uncomfortable Nissen huts, the need for fresh crews had reached its peak.

There are other less likely possibilities these being R.A.F. Wigsley, a satellite of Swinderby, which was 7½ miles south of Lincoln (1654 H.C.U. codes UG and JF) or R.A.F.Winthorpe very near Newark (1661 H.C.U. codes GP and KB). The last of these stations is now the home of Newark Air Museum, which has an artefact display centred around the vital role the airfield played in the training of 5 Group aircrew.

Preparation here would have been intense and certainly included aspects of night navigation flying, fighter affiliation and sessions on the bombing ranges. Losses on such units were heavy, as novice aircrew were pushed up to, and sometimes beyond their limits. They surely must have found flying at night in British weather over a 'blacked out' countryside far removed from, and more dangerous than, the open spaces of Canadian prairie or Texan grassland, where many had learnt their basic skills. This course would have lasted five weeks, one in the classroom and four providing 40 hours of flying.

A further problem encountered was that of shortage of suitable aircraft. Front line bombers were in short supply and so much of this work was being done using Short Stirlings, a point supported by Mr. H Priestley, a flight engineer who flew a total of 37 operations with 207 Squadron. He was transferred to Wigsley on 7/7/44 where he served as an instructor on these aircraft. Further evidence is also the lack of air accidents involving Lancasters on the H.C.U.'s during 1944.

It is interesting to note that the Air Officer Commanding, Air Vice Marshal The Hon. Ralph Cochrane made the following comments in 'V' Group News July 1944 (No. 24):

'During July, No. 51 Base raised their total figures once more and passed out 150 trained crews. No.5 L.F.S. completed a second month in succession with no flying accidents and I again congratulate them on a fine achievement.'

I think it is obvious from the above, training could be hazardous and that crews passing through the system had already endured more than most people realised. In all a total in excess of 8,000 aircrew perished during their time at training bases, a figure representing 14% of Bomber Command losses.

After completing their stint at the H.C.U. the next and final stage of preparation was a brief visit to a "Lancaster Finishing School", (L.F.S.) where time was spent converting to the Lancaster aircraft they would fly on operational service.
At this stage we can be more sure about where the crew were stationed, by now they had been assigned to the 5 Group Finishing School at R.A.F. Syerston, an airfield opened in December 1940 and situated about 10 miles north east of Nottingham, between the A46 Newark to Nottingham road and the river Trent. The school had been operating here since January 1944 and closed at the end of March 1945. (Aircraft codes used were RC and CE).

This course was short, and depending largely on the weather could have been completed in between 10 days and a fortnight, with only about 15 hours spent flying. It therefore seems likely that they would have missed the bizarre accident which happened at this station on 27 May when Lancaster W4383 managed to land on top of W4258. It was no doubt still a talking point when they arrived.

Occasionally crews were 'blooded' from these training bases and were involved in 'nickel' raids (pamphlet dropping) or diversionary 'spoof' raids aimed at confusing the enemy and so reducing casualties in the main bomber force. Whether P/O McIntosh and his crew were called on for these activities isn't known.

Using R.A.F. Form 540 as a reference it would appear the crew left here on June 16 1944, had a short period of leave and arrived at their new home R.A.F. Spilsby ready for active service on the 20 June 1944.

CHAPTER 3: FOAMRANGE SPILSBY AND OPS

R.A.F. Spilsby, codename 'Foamrange', became operational in October 1943 when the personnel of 207 Squadron transferred from their previous home at R.A.F. Langer. From all accounts it was not a popular move. Langer was a well established airfield with some creature comforts, near to civilisation. Spilsby on the other hand was still incomplete when the move took place, it was near to nowhere in particular and high on the Lincolnshire Wolds. Even the buildings left something to be desired, consisting mainly of temporary brick, and hutting provided by Nissen, Laing and the British Concrete Federation. It was not a home from home.

Many servicemen and women would have arrived at Spilsby via Firsby Junction, a small village railway station, now long closed, but sited about 2 miles away from the entrance to the airfield. It was part of the Great Northern Railway network and was on a line which ran south to Boston and north to Skegness and Grimsby. The majority of the crew arrived on the 20 June with Pilot Officer McIntosh joining them a day later. Early priorities were no doubt to do with finding a billet and the crew would have been assigned to accommodation on one of the dispersed sites in and around the village of Great Steeping, but their exact quarters are not known, other than that, as an officer, McIntosh would not have been living with the rest of the crew.

They were obviously given a few quiet days to find their feet in this new environment and would have been heartened to learn that in the preceding month only one aircraft, that of F/O Briggs and crew (EM-N ME678), had been lost on operations. During this time they were allocated to 'A' Flight and hopefully had some opportunity to gain extra hours in the air. P/O McIntosh, Sgt. Little and Sgt. Shannon all flew a sortie to Wesseling on the night of 21/22 June to gain experience of 'ops'. We do know that Shannon flew as a second bomb aimer with the following crew:

F/O Oakes, E.   Sgt. Brundle, A.D.   F/Sgt,Chesworth,G.D.
W/O Ainsworth, G.W.R.   Sgt. Shannon, G.R.   Sgt. Lee, A.J.
Sgt, Butterworth,   Sgt. Hanson,

Their report for the action is as follows:

BOMBING ATTACK WESSELING

UP   23.29   DOWN   03.46

Bomb Load 1x4000lb. M. 4x500lbG.P. L.D.37B. 12X500lb. G.P. Weather conditions: 10/10ths cloud, target identified by Markers and H2S. Bombed at 01.43 hrs. from 17,000ft on heading of 130 degrees T. at 165 m.p.h. I.A.S. More glow on cloud as attack progressed suggesting fires burning below.

SORTIE COMPLETED.

Sgt. Little accompanied the crew below on the same operation:

P/O N Owen   F/Sgt. E.G.S. Scutt   P/O L. Levy
Sgt. S.W.G. Little   W/O G.M. Brown   P/O A.L. Sale
Sgt. P.W. Corley   Sgt. R.W.H. Smith

This crew was very experienced and nearing the end of their tour, as can be seen from the comment below, taken from squadron records:

'4.7.44 P/0 N Owen's crew did not fly on this operation. Although it was not announced at the time, their first tour was completed on the last operation. They had made 36 sorties.'

Wesseling was a synthetic oil plant and the predicted clear bombing conditions were very wide of the mark when the force encountered 10/10 low cloud over the target. Generally the bombing was inaccurate and damage slight, only hampering oil production for a short time. It had been an extremely costly night with 37 Lancasters being lost, the following 207 crews had been part of the price paid:

Pilot Officer E.A. Goodman EM-U DV 360 Lancaster 1
Pilot Officer C J. Solly EM-M LL 937 Lancaster 1
Flying Officer A.V.D. Corless R.C.A.F. EM-W ME 683 Lancaster 1
Flight Lieutenant F.W. Gallagher D.S.O. EM- I ME 829 Lancaster 1
Flying Officer T.T Smart D.F.C. EM-L LM 578 Lancaster 111

Losses from the above crews were as follows:
Dead 27   Prisoners 5   Evaders of capture 4.

No doubt our 'sprog' (novice) crew would have been most interested to hear the thoughts of their crewmates about this raid. From the report above it appears to have been 'incident free', but even so the losses of 5 experienced crews, mostly by night fighter action, must have brought home very clearly the dangers they were about to face. Squadron strength had also been reduced. They would have realised their own initiation was imminent.

It was to come on 24 June when the crew saw that they were on standby for 'ops'. How they felt is not known but it can be imagined that a range of emotions from 'blind panic' to excitement must have been experienced during the course of the day while they waited to attend briefing at the administration site; just outside the main airfield entrance to the west along the road leading to Halton Holgate.

The target was to be Pommereval north of Paris which was one of seven German flying bomb sites to be attacked that night. The weather over the target was clear and moonlit and the majority of aircraft lost to night fighter attack operating with the help of searchlights. Early arrivals over the target had an easier time and were able to bomb and leave before the defences responded. When they did, both heavy and light flak were accurate and claimed several casualties. There was more flak over the Dieppe area and four intersecting searchlights had to be overflown near the coast. These were being switched on and off at regular intervals.

The McIntosh crew did not have a quiet introduction as can be seen from their report which is reproduced below, taken from the squadron operational record book:

24/25.6.44

Lancaster 111 ND 555

P/O McIntosh P.C.	Sgt. Grint J.R.	F/Sgt. Little S.W.G.
Sgt. Shannon G.R.	Sgt. Beech J.	Sgt. Bateman L.D
Sgt. Burton W.R.		

Up. 22.42 Down. 01.49

BOMBING ATTACK POMMEREVAL

Bomb load 16x500 M.C T.D. 025 2x500 lb M.C.L.D.36 hours. Target attacked in clear conditions with some base at 00.08 hours from 7900 feet on heading of 035 degrees. T at I.A.S. of 170 m.p.h. Identified by Green T.I.s. No observations made as aircraft was attacked by twin engined enemy aircraft immediately after bombing.

SORTIE COMPLETED.

The following, more detailed account of the action the McIntosh crew experienced over the target area is taken from P.R.O. document AIR 28/722 and is reproduced below unamended:

'Those who bombed early found the defences apparently quite unprepared and were able to bomb and leave the target area before the flak started. This was only intermittent and consisted of both heavy and light flak. This was less than had been expected, but it was accurate and several aircraft were seen to be shot down by it. There were only one or two searchlights in the area and four intersecting at the coast. These flicked on and off at regular intervals. There was also some flak in the Dieppe area, but not much.

There were a number of fighter sightings, as well as five combats. P/0 P. McIntosh, who was on his first operational solo, was unfortunate enough to be attacked twice. The first time was just as he approached the target. His gunners, Sgt. L. Bateman and Sgt. W. Burton, sighted a Me. 109 coming in on the starboard bow. They fired, but could not observe the result, so make no claim. There was no return of fire.

The enemy aircraft was shaken off, so P/0. P. McIntosh went in and made his bombing run. He had only just completed this and dropped his bombs when a twin-engined aircraft was seen on the port quarter. His gunners at once opened fire, while the pilot immediately went into a corkscrew. The fighter was again shaken off, but again no claim can be made. His photograph, of course, was spoilt, as also was that of P/0 N. Ferguson who had to go into a sudden dive immediately after bombing, in order to avoid a collision with another Lancaster.'

Nothing is known of crew activity for the next couple of days until they were again 'on' for a sortie to Marquis Mimoyecques during the night of 27/28 June. Personnel were the same as for the previous flight, take off was at 23.15 and landing at 03.05, the aircraft used on this occasion was Lancaster 111 NE 168.

Details from the record book are as follows:

BOMBING ATTACK MARQUIS MIMOYECQUES

Bomb load llxl000 lb M.C 2x500 M.C.Inst. 2x500 M.C. L.D. Target which was identified by Red T.I.was bombed at 00.55 hours

SORTIE COMPLETED.

FOAMRANGE: SPILSBY AND 'OPS'

To use the terminology of the time this operation appears to have been a 'milk run' for the crew and everything had gone to plan. Maybe it boosted confidence a little to realize that not every flight was to be as demanding as their first, but of course they would have realised they still had a very long way to go if they were to complete their tour of operations.

The above target was another 'V weapon site, but this time the base of the V3 weapon, a 25 barrel long range gun, capable of shelling London. It had been attacked on the previous evening, but the job still needed finishing off. Other attacks that evening were against railway yards at Vaires and Vitry, the former being severely damaged but the latter only being hit at the western end of the site.

All in all it had been a successful night for Bomber Command. Attacks had been relatively successful and less than one percent of the aircraft involved had been lost.

The crew were rested until they were called upon for another attack on 4 July. It is likely that they were one of the 19 crews detailed for operations on the 1 July, but even though the weather was fine in Lincolnshire, the attack was 'scrubbed'. A similar problem arose on the 2 July when 19 crews were again 'stood down' after briefing, but time was used for H2S radar training and flights at the bombing ranges.

Which crews were involved in these aborted raids I'm not sure, but the pressure and expectation they were made to suffer in the build up must have been hard to reconcile when the 'op' was cancelled. No doubt, outwardly, relief was the obvious sign, but as in many conflicts the psychological damage done by announcing and then cancelling an attack must have wreaked havoc in the minds of those involved.

Throughout the latter part of June German night fighter defences had been being strengthened in France and now covered the area S.W. of Paris as far as the Loire and the neighbourhood of Tours. For attacks forthcoming in July this meant that areas of occupied territory now defended by night fighter 'Gruppes' had to be considered to include areas east of the Greenwich meridian and north of 47N. Our crew were probably unaware that from this stage onward the risks were about to increase, and the ratio of bombers lost was to be 3:1 in favour of fighter attack over flak.

On 3 July nothing was planned and crews could relax. The weather was again fine and training exercises were carried out. On this day Group Captain W. E. Cheshire was posted abroad and Group Captain S.N.V. Harris took overall control of the station.

There was activity again on the 4 July as the armourers laboured in the bomb stores. Yet again 19 aircraft were being prepared to attack and among the crews detailed to fly them was that of the newly promoted Flying Officer McIntosh. No records have been found regarding this, but I have been told by a veteran 207 aircrew member that this was an automatic step up the ladder. Apparently a Pilot Officer became a Flying Officer 6 months after gaining his commission, which, if it is right in this case, points to the fact that 'Mac' must have been granted his commission at the very end of 1943 or the start of 1944.

It is also known that Ross Shannon was at some point promoted to Flight Sergeant. Throughout his time on the squadron he is always listed as Sergeant, but on the Runnymede Memorial his rank is Flight Sergeant, which points to the fact that he'd held the lower rank for one year and also received automatic promotion.

The sortie scheduled for the 4/5 July was carried out under a full moon and like those previously tackled was against a flying bomb site. This time the target was St. Leu D'esserent, an underground store built into caves in a limestone hillside thirty five miles north east of Paris. The aim of this attack was to cut communications to the site and block the cave entrances. 1000 lb. bombs were used and the resulting damage indicated only a partially successful raid. Enemy fighters were again very active, being guided by searchlights, light beacons and the occasional use of radio beacons. They intercepted the bomber stream and a total of 13 Lancasters were shot down, two of these coming from 207 Squadron:

FOAMRANGE: SPILSBY AND 'OPS'

Pilot Officer J.H. Wilson EM-G LM 125 Lancaster 1

Flight Sergeant J.W. Gibbs EM-Z ND 570 Lancaster 111.

Of the 14 crew aboard the 2 aircraft 13 perished with only the bomb aimer from the Gibbs crew surviving to become a prisoner of war.

Other operations were taking place during the night in question, and there were high hopes for a new communications jamming device being used for the first time. This was codenamed 'Jostle' and was carried by Fortresses of 100 Group. It was a high powered airborne jammer designed for use against communications in the high frequency band and was directed against night fighter interceptors using a running commentary to find their prey. The effect was difficult to assess but the percentage losses don't seem to be greatly reduced.

After a trouble free attack 5 days earlier, the crew were presumably very hopeful they could repeat this feat. They were again flying NE 168, a good omen? Squadron records for their sortie are as follows:

> Took off 23.45   Landed 02.55.

BOMBING ATTACK ST LEU D'ESSERENT

> Bomb load llxl000 lb M.C. 4x500 lb G.P.
> Target attacked at 01.35 hours.

One M.E. 109 shot down. Rear gunner and flight engineer injured. Aircraft landed at WOODBRIDGE.

SORTIE COMPLETED.

For the above sortie Bateman appears to have been missing and was replaced by Flight Sergeant G.E. Barker in the mid upper gun turret. No reasons for this can be found, but Bateman was to return for the next flight.

The moving report of what happened to the crew on this sortie is reproduced below. It is unamended and is taken from P.R.O. document AIR 28/722:

'It was on the return that the real trouble began. Numerous sightings of aircraft on fire are reported. In many cases the cause was unknown, but in those cases where it was possible to state the cause, by far the greater number of casualties were due to fighter action.

A few minutes after bombing, P/O. McIntosh's crew in "F" were attacked by a Me. 109. Both aircraft fired and the Rear Gunner of the Lancaster (Sgt. W. Burton) was injured in the face. Both gunners had been firing but the Rear Gunner was blinded with blood and had to leave off. The tail plane was damaged, the port elevator was shot away and the starboard outer petrol tank was holed. Control was difficult and the pilot had to use force to keep the controls in position. Later he had to hold them back with his knees.

Sgt. G.R. Shannon, the Air Bomber, went back to do what he could for the wounded gunner. He carried him out of his turret and did what First Aid was possible, but Sgt. W. Burton had lost a lot of blood and he presently became unconscious. Sgt. Shannon meanwhile took his place in the rear turret and did what he could to help the pilot by swinging the turret in such a way as to help with the balance of the aircraft. As the doors would not close, he was in danger of being sucked out, but he continued to do this nevertheless.

Meanwhile the fighter had again come into the the attack. F/Sgt. G.E. Barker, the Mid-Upper Gunner, at once fired and continued firing until he had shot down the fighter, which went down in flames and is therefore claimed as destroyed.

P/O McIntosh headed for a layer of cloud, but before he could reach this both F/Sgt. G.E. Barker and Sgt. G.R. Shannon observed another enemy aircraft in the neighbourhood. They watched this anxiously until they entered cloud cover and then the fighter dropped flares all round them and seemed to be trying to contact them. In this he was fortunately unsuccessful for though F/Sgt. G.E. Barker was ready for him, it was entirely impossible for P/O McIntosh to carry out any sort of evasive action. He was able to fly in cloud for the greater part of the way home and after it gave out the Pilot decided to come down and fly low over the sea so as to minimise the risk of further fighter attack. By this time the aircraft was becoming increasingly difficult to control, and the Flight Engineer (Sgt. J.R. Grint) was helping the pilot to struggle with the controls. P/O McIntosh suggested using the rubber oxygen tube as a rope so Sgt. J.R. Grint fixed this up so as to hold the controls in position. This broke, but he soon remedied this and succeeded in making it hold. The Wireless Operator (Sgt. J. Beech) attempted to send a message giving information as to their position and their difficulties, but at this time the aircraft was too low for him to do this. Later, when the Pilot climbed, he was able to send a message which was received at Base just before "F" was due back there. This message stated that "F" would be landing at Woodbridge as the aircraft was damaged and the Rear Gunner injured. Needless to say, further news was anxiously awaited from Woodbridge.

The captain had decided to try and land his damaged aircraft on the Emergency Landing ground at Woodbridge. This gave him plenty of space for landing and enabled him to obtain medical aid for Sgt. Burton sooner than if he attempted to return to Base. He decided on this course in preference to ordering the crew to bale out on account of the Rear Gunner who by this time was unconscious. The crew were anxious that he should attempt a landing as he himself could never have baled out, as it was quite impossible to trim the aircraft and to keep it straight and level for a sufficient length of time. He therefore obtained a course from the Navigator F/Sgt. Little and headed for Woodbridge. He then ordered the crew to crash stations except for Sgt. J.R. Grint whose help was necessary in landing the aircraft and proceeded to land. He made a good landing, but it was inevitably somewhat bumpy and Sgt. J.R. Grint unfortunately slipped and injured his foot. The rest of the crew were unhurt. This crew has added one more to the long list of episodes in which a determined and capable crew show what can be done by co-operation and initiative to avert what might so easily have become a disaster, and to turn it into a success.'

Woodbridge was an airfield with widened and lengthened runways situated in Suffolk. At the time it's main purpose was to provide an emergency landing facility for pilots with either damaged aircraft or injured crew to land quickly and safely without having to take the added risks or time involved in returning to their own squadron base. There were few comforts at 'The Bone Yard' (Woodbridge) and airmen stranded there often found themselves arriving at a local 'Bed and Breakfast' in full flying kit during the small hours, before returning to their squadrons later in the day. How our crew got back to Spilsby is not known. In some instances airmen travelled by train using a travel warrant, sometimes in a lorry sent to collect them, some even presumably flew back if damage had been repaired quickly.

The next 12 days pose something of a mystery. The McIntosh crew appear to have 'gone to ground' and although aircraft from 207 flew on several operations, they were not involved in any of them. Ron Winton, from the Squadron Association, feels that they were probably sent on 'survivors' leave' following their last 'op' and would have been told to report back for duty when either replacement men or machines, maybe both, became available again. I do know that, during his spell at Spilsby, Ross did make some visits to the Hall family in Boston. Vin, my aunt mentioned earlier, has clear recollections of these. She knows he was on active service during these visits as she remembers him talking about it, but not in great detail, and also that he had insignia on his uniform, presumably the air bomber's brevet on his blouse. Her initial recall was that he was now a pilot but she wasn't sure. What she was sure of was that he was flying, and of feeling concerned for him because he was such a quiet and gentle sort of boy. Whether any of these visits took place during this lull in their active service we don't know for certain, but what we do know is that they provided the last chance for anyone from Browns Road to see this young man who for a fleeting time had become almost a member of the family.

Life, in fact life and death, continued at the airfield. On the 7 July the weather was fine and 16 crews were detailed to pay another visit to St. Leu D'esserent. This time the defences were even better primed to meet them and 5 squadron aircraft failed to return. These are listed below:

Flying Officer C.E. Stamp EM-Y LM 129 Lancaster 1
Flight Sergeant K.A. Boyce EM-N LM 218 Lancaster I
Flying Officer A. Alderton EM-J ME 805 Lancaster 1
Flying Officer T.J. Hardley EM—V ND 567 Lancaster 111
Pilot Officer M.N. Milner EM-B ND 886 Lancaster 111.

Of the 35 men in these crews, 19 were killed, 7 taken prisoner and the surprisingly large number of 9 became evaders.

Cloudy weather followed for the next few days and several operations were planned, crews were put on stand by only for sorties to be 'scrubbed'. On the 12 July the skies cleared and 12 crews attacked Chalindrey. They all returned safely but bad weather closed in on Lincolnshire and their landings were diverted to other airfields.

The 13 July was wet during the morning but cleared in the afternoon, an attack was planned and then cancelled, but the following day seven 207 crews took off on a sortie to Villeneuve St. George. These were railway marshalling yards, which were damaged even though much of the bombing fell wide of the target. Crews all got home without problem and Squadron Leader Pattinson completed his second tour of operations when he landed after this flight.

Looking at the operational record books for this period the number of crews being detailed for sorties had decreased dramatically. Whereas only 10 days previously the squadron had regularly been providing nineteen aircraft they were now working on a maximum of twelve.

I wonder if this supports the idea of our 'sprog' crew being given leave. New aircraft were delivered to Spilsby on the 10 July, PB 293 and PB 294 being among them. Presumably these were needed to replace the five aircraft lost on the 7/8 of the month.

On the 15 July thirteen aircraft were initially detailed to fly, but this was later reduced to six with one reserve. Six aircraft attacked Nevers railway yards and Flight Lieutenant Jones and his crew (EM-S ME 807) were all killed when they came down at Lignieres de Touraine. This crew was unusual in that eight men were on board instead of the normal seven. Although it's not clear it would seem possible that Flying Officer Dalgleish was a newcomer who had been sent with Jones to gain some experience before taking his own crew into action, a point raised earlier regarding P/O McIntosh. This practice of novice pilots being given a flight or two with more experienced 'skippers' was known as a 'second dickie' trip, sadly Dalgleish's first taste of action was also his last and the 6 young men who had waited for his return were left without a pilot. This made them a 'headless' crew and would mean their return to training where a new pilot would have been found.

Several crews on this sortie reported seeing an air accident over the target area when 2 bombers collided, both were seen to disintegrate. As there were only 2 planes lost it can be safely assumed that F/L Jones crashed with the 467 Squadron aircraft of F/L Murphy who had taken off from Waddington at 22.19 in Lancaster PO-B ME 851. All 15 aircrew involved were killed.

The next 2 days were fine and on the 18 July 13 aircraft attacked German troop concentrations at Caen in France. It was a successful raid with no losses and had been organized in conjunction with the U.S.A.A.F. which enabled over 2000 planes to take part in the offensive. It was on this raid that the McIntosh crew reappear, having been rested for 12 days.

Briefing for the Caen attack took place at midnight and our crew took off at 03.55 on the 18 July. For this sortie the crew had Sergeant T.J. Dawson (or Dowson) as a replacement gunner. If squadron details are taken literally he was in the mid upper turret and Bateman had moved to the rear. This could have happened but it's just as likely their names were reversed when a busy typist was filling in details.

Squadron records make it clear the flight was untroubled, and the details recorded are very matter of fact.

Take off 03.55   Landed 07.21

BOMBING ATTACK CAEN

> Bomb load 11x1000 lb, 4x500 lb.
> Weather hazy otherwise clear. Ground detail visible.
> Target identified visually, canal could be seen.
> Bombed at 05.48 hours from 9000 ft. heading 190'(T)
> I A S 160 m.p.h. M.P.I. of two yellow T I's bombed
> as ordered.

SORTIE COMPLETED.

Having landed at 07.21 the crew must have been surprised to find out they were required to fly again later the same day. This time the target was a rail junction at Revigny Sur Ornain, the objective of the raid being to cut the flow of German men and machines heading towards the allied front line now pushing forward from the Normandy beach head. The bombing was carried out successfully but only at great expense when the raid was intercepted by enemy single engined freelance fighters from St. Dizier airfield. Twenty four Lancasters from those dispatched by various squadrons were lost.

The McIntosh crew managed to avoid the carnage over France that evening because they returned early due to problems with the aircraft. Squadron records are as follows:

BOMBING ATTACK REVIGNY

Take off 22.56　　　　Landed 00.20

Bomb load　　10x1000 lb M.C.　　2x500 lb 2x500 lb G.P.

　　　　　　36 hours delay.　　Early return.

Jettisoned 10x1000 lb M.C 2x500 lb　2x500 lb

36 hour delay 53.16N 43.11E.

Starboard inner engine tending to feather. Also general electrical defect.

SORTIE NOT COMPLETED

The landing time given appears to be wrong. It is more likely to be 02.00.

A little extra detail can be given about this operation from this extract taken from the Station Record Book:

'F/O McIntosh returned early. His starboard inner engine kept feathering and there was some doubt as to whether the others were reliable so he decided to turn back from the Channel islands area.'

It's also worth mentioning that for the first time in their tour Sergeant Joseph Grint was not with them; his position as flight engineer being taken by Sergeant Briggs. The reasons for this are unknown, Grint had flown with the crew on the sortie to Caen earlier on the 18 July but was unable to join them only 15 hours later. No mention of injury, in fact no record of anything amiss was made after Caen so just what was the matter will have to remain a mystery.

The aircraft losses from 207 squadron amounted to the following on this night:

Flying Officer N.L. Weekes EM-T ME 681 Lancaster 1

Flying Officer J.G. Dallen EM-E ME 814 Lancaster I

Flying Officer W.R. McNaughton EM-C PD 210 Lancaster 1

Of the 21 aircrew aboard 19 were killed and 2 evaded capture. The McNaughton crew had arrived at Spilsby on the same day as the McIntosh crew. Their tour had lasted less than one month when they were shot down at 02.04 by a F.W.190 fighter as they returned home from the target. The only survivor from the attack was Sergeant John Chapple, the wireless operator, who was blown out of the aircraft when the fuel tanks exploded. He survived the ensuing parachute fall but dislocated his right leg on landing and then spent six weeks being sheltered by Pierre Lanhanque, the baker in the village of Marson, until the American Army arrived on 27 August.

His crewmates' bodies were all recovered and buried locally, but it took six days to find the remains of the pilot, Ross McNaughton. His body was eventually discovered in an oat field where he had fallen from the aircraft without his parachute.

Just before John Chapple returned to England a Mass was said at the church in St. Germain-la-Ville, where his colleagues were buried. The church was overflowing and Sergeant Chapple was most 'touched' by the sincere gratitude expressed by the local people.

Flying Officer Dallen's aircraft was also brought down by a night fighter and was seen to crash from another aircraft at 01.34 as it headed along the last short leg into the target. The only survivor from this crew was Flight Sergeant Len Aitken, the bomb aimer, who subsequently spent some time living in woods with the Maquis fighters before heading for Switzerland with another evader called Reg Hillborne. Their intended escape failed and they were later involved with a British S.A.S. group dropped behind enemy lines and tasked to disrupt German troop and supply movements. After many adventures they eventually reached the allied beach head and were ferried back to England by landing craft on 7 September.

There were no survivors from the aircraft piloted by Flying Officer Weekes. It crashed on fire into a field near the village of Chacun Maine and was also a victim of night fighter attack. The aircraft hit the ground with its bombs still on board and left a crater ten feet deep. Part of a broken propellor from this bomber was used in the memorial erected to the crew and still stands today to perpetuate their memory. The crew were only on their fourth operation.

FOAMRANGE: SPILSBY AND 'OPS'

Returning to the McIntosh crew, there may be a link between this failed sortie to Revigny and the crew's last flight which will be discussed in more detail in the next chapter. As can be seen from the squadron records the crew jettisoned their bomb load at 53.16N and 43.11E before landing back at Spilsby. This would appear to be a point well out to sea directly east of Anderby Creek and I suspect it could have been a designated 'safe area' or 'drop zone'. The eastings given must be wrong, with the minutes being 43 and not the degrees. This would then give a location 15 miles off the Lincolnshire coast. Such areas would have been known to allied sailors as places to stay well clear of, particularly at a time when Bomber Command were airborne. In fact at any time, as unwanted bombs were often time delayed and therefore explosions could in theory have taken place without warning during day or night. As already said there could be a link to later actions but I will mention this in the next chapter.

The crew were stood down on the 19 July but 7 others attacked Tiverny, another V weapon launch site. Lessons had obviously been learnt since the recent disasters over Revigny and this time a fighter escort ensured all returned to base. On the 20 July squadron aircraft attacked a railway junction at Coutrai, with all 11 dispatched returning safely to Spilsby, but 9 crews being lost from other squadrons. The weather in Lincolnshire was fine for the next few days but the fourteen crews on 'stand by' had operations cancelled on both the 21 July and the 22 July. Training, cross country and fighter affiliation work was carried out instead.

On the 23 July fifteen aircraft were detailed to fly but only seven were eventually required to attack the 'U' boat yards at Kiel. These took off at about 22.30 and all got back, although seven aircraft from other squadrons were brought down. It seems likely that the seven crews stood down on the night of the 23 July were intended for the first night attack on Donges. Plans had been changed and they would take their turn over this target on the following night, Monday 24/Tuesday 25 July.

Chapter 4: THE LAST SORTIE

The crew were joined on this operation by Sergeant Arthur William Smith who was continuing the list of 'pool' gunners to have occupied the rear turret since the loss of Sergeant Burton. Smith had only been at Spilsby for a maximum of twelve days and there's no evidence to support him being a regular member of an established crew on 207 Squadron.

The target for this raid was an oil refinery and storage depot at Donges, which is situated in western France at the mouth of the River Loire, not far from St. Nazaire. One end of the installation had been attacked the previous night with no losses from the 119 aircraft which took part. All these aircraft came from 6 and 8 Group and comprised 100 Halifaxes, 14 Lancasters and 5 Mosquitoes. The bombing had taken place in good visibility with severe damage being caused to the target area, damage which included an oil tanker being hit and subsequently capsizing.

The above information would no doubt have been passed on to them during their briefing at the administration site during the afternoon or early evening of 24 July. On the same day nine other more experienced crews were being prepared to attack Stuttgart; the first sortie on a south German target for about 3 months.

The McIntosh crew and five others, less experienced like themselves, had been assigned to the easier attack on Donges. There must have been a near audible sigh of relief from these 'sprog' (newcomer) crews when they heard the news, and I suspect groans of dismay from those faced with the more daunting task in Germany. Whether or not the lack of attacks for some time mentioned above was responsible we don't know, but the defences mistook the raid for one of deep penetration on France and as a consequence only night fighter group 4JD were sent to find the bomber stream heading for Stuttgart.

THE LAST SORTIE

It had been another fine, typically summer's day, the fifth on the trot, high pressure over eastern England guaranteed late sunshine and as the crew were ferried out to their aircraft just before 21.00 they must have felt that their 'lot' was improving. Not only had they been told the 'op' was a milk run (easy target), but they had also been allocated a Lancaster 111, code EM-G, airframe PB 294; an aircraft which had arrived at Spilsby as a brand new machine on 10 July. This 'Lanc' was 14 days old, surely it would be in pristine condition and afford them an easy run there and back, proving more reliable and responsive then some of the heavily 'used' examples they'd sampled in their 'ops' up to now. After trawling through squadron records between the date of delivery and this sortie we can only find evidence for this aircraft having flown once operationally prior to the 24 July. This was when F/Lt. Harding and crew took it on a successful and trouble free raid to Coutrai on 20/21 July. It may have flown more, but several entries in the operations book lack aircraft numbers so we cannot be certain of this.

The bomb load now stored in the belly of 'G' George was as follows:

11 x 1000 lb medium capacity
2 x 500 lb medium capacity
2 x 500 lb medium capacity fitted with 6 hour delay fuses.

These latter weapons designed to go off hours after landing on the ground. For the time being the deadly cargo which nestled below the crew would not be at the front of their minds. Final checks were carried out and at about 21.30 'G' George left it's dispersal and joined the perimeter track making its way to the end of the runway for take off. It was airborne, according to squadron records at 21.50. They had left 'mother earth' for the final time.

As can be seen from the squadron report below the crew were acting as windfinders on this operation. This was seen as an aid to navigation and used the 'Broadcast Wind' or 'Zephyr System'. Navigators would obtain fixes using H2S radar and from these calculate wind strength and direction information which was transmitted back to England in encoded form every thirty minutes. These findings were averaged out at Bomber Command headquarters and fifteen minutes later re-broadcast to other bombers in the stream. In theory at least this should have had the effect of keeping the whole stream more tightly packed but there is plenty of evidence to suggest it was not always a success.

Reading between the lines, it appears that the McIntosh crew were no longer being regarded as raw novices. The windfinder duty was usually given to seasoned crews who could be relied upon to help less experienced colleagues, and they must have been by this time well versed in the use of H2S radar. Their role may also explain why they were aboard a new aircraft as it was necessarily one fitted with this equipment, and further points to the fact that this aircraft may well have been used mainly for H2S training rather than 'ops.' since arriving on the squadron 2 weeks previously.

The route taken outbound to the target is not known but using information sourced from similar operations of the time it is likely that the general course flew S.S.W. over central England before crossing the coast in the area of Weymouth and Portland Bill.

At this point let us return to P.R.O. document AIR 28/722:

'The aircraft detailed for the Donges attack took off about 3/4 hour after the Stuttgart force, except for F/O McIntosh and F/O J.W.G.Hodgkinson, who were windfinders and who therefore took off twenty minutes before the others.

The outward trip was uneventful and the target was identified without difficulty by means of the red and green T.Is. Some crews saw ground detail in the light of the flares. On the previous night, Halifaxes and Lancasters of 6 Group had made a satisfactory attack on one end of this important oil refinery so the ninety eight Lancasters and four Mosquitoes of 5 Group were to attack the other. This they achieved with considerable success. The red oboe markers went down punctually and these were backed up by green T.Is. Most crews bombed on the green T.Is. but a large explosion caused so much smoke that one crew was obliged to bomb on the glow of fires seen through it, T.Is. having been seen in their neighbourhood earlier.

There was some light flak and very little heavy. An aircraft was seen coned in searchlights while light flak was pumped up at it, but all the 207 Squadron aircraft managed to avoid the searchlights. F/O J.D. Ready's crew sighted a fighter just after bombing, but the pilot put the aircraft into a corkscrew and eventually the enemy aircraft was shaken off. F/LT. M.F.C. Harding's Wireless Operator, W/O M. Savage, reported an indication on Fishpond of an aircraft closing in on them. By the speed at which it travelled it seemed likely to be a fighter, but it was shaken off by a corkscrew before visual contact had been made. Apart from this, there were no fighters reported and, apart from the fact that F/O J.D. Ready's crew had some trouble with various minor defects, the return to Base was uneventful for five of the six crews.

The sixth was F/O McIntosh in "G". He called up over Base with the others, but added:- "Dangerous hang-up, am going out to jettison. Back in an hour". That is the last that was heard from him. Group have plots which suggest that he was on his way back, and the Royal Observer Corps report seeing an aircraft go down in the sea approximately five miles from the coast. A.S.S.R. took immediate action and an aircraft was over the scene of the accident 20 minutes after it occurred. A high-speed launch from Grimsby was sent out, as well as the Skegness Lifeboat. As the aircraft did not catch fire till a short while after falling into the sea, it was hoped that they might have escaped, but such was not the case. Two or three bodies were seen floating, but only the body of F/O McIntosh was picked up, as the others sank before they could be picked up. He had been killed by a blow on the head, and it seems likely that for some unknown reason the aircraft, without warning, suddenly became completely uncontrollable and dived, giving the pilot no chance to ditch properly.

THE LAST SORTIE

The pilot's Mae West was not inflated, neither were those of the other bodies seen. The landing wheels and various pieces of the aircraft have been collected. Only two other aircraft were lost on this target. F/O McIntosh was on his seventh sortie.'

The five other 207 crews detailed were as follows:

F/O J.W. Hodgkinson	PB	293	UP	22.00	DOWN	04.12
F/O C.H. Coulter	LM	535	UP	22.21	DOWN	04.05
F/Lt. M.F.C. Harding	PD	226	UP	22.20	DOWN	04.08
F/O D.W. Ready	PD	217	UP	22.23	DOWN	04.02
F/O R.C. Davies	LM	671	UP	22.18	DOWN	04.07

Times of bombing ranged from 01.41 to 01.50 and heights from 8500 feet to 11000 feet. There is no mention of any of the crews having problems with flak. It would appear to have been a very straightforward operation as they'd expected.

Of the 35 crew members in the above aircraft 12 were later lost. F/Lt. Harding and crew crashed on 26 August 1944 tasked to attack Darmstadt in PD 216 EM-J, and F/O Ready and crew went missing without trace on 16 October 1944 while on a 'gardening' sortie in NG 143 EM-R.

Along with the McIntosh crew the two aircraft from other squadrons lost over Donges were:

Lancaster 111 PA 968 VN-S 50 Squadron T/O Skellingthorpe 22.18

PlO C.B. Haaland R.C.A.F.
Sgt. R. Craig
Sgt. J.L. Nelson R.C.A.F.
F/O S.D. Sullivan R.C.A.F.
Sgt. W.J.B. Doughty
Sgt. N. Gronbeck R.C.A.F.
Sgt. Finch R.C.A.F.

THE LAST SORTIE

Lancaster 111 LM 643 PG-E 619 Squadron
T/O Dunholme Lodge 22.27

F/O R.W. Orbell
Sgt. J.R. Ward
Sgt. J.J. Kommes R.C.A.F.
F/S D.M. Murphy R.C.A.F.
Sgt. G.H. Lucas
Sgt. J.R. Scott
Sgt. S. Sinclair.

All these young men perished and are buried in France. The Haaland crew crashed at Pontchateau 19 miles north east of St. Nazaire and are buried there in the communal cemetery. Orbell's aircraft came down at Montoir de Bretagne, 6 km north east of St. Nazaire. Murphy rests at Montoir de Bretagne, five others in Escoublac Ia Baule and Sergeant Ward is interred in Pornic war cemetery. Why these burials are so spread out is not clear but it could be that some crew unsuccessfully attempted to bale out or that the aircraft disintegrated in the air before crashing due to damage sustained by the flak attack. It seems likely that one of these crews was in the aircraft coned by searchlights and shot at with light flak, but there is no way of telling which one.

Wing Commander Woodroffe, master bomber on the raid who co-ordinated the attacks from the air over the target, felt the operation had been a success and according to his own and other contemporary reports, the target was 'devastated', a point supported by the fact that Bomber Command never felt it necessary to attack this depot again. The following report from '5 Group News' No. 24 July 1944 reads as follows:
'104 aircraft from all bases were detailed for the attack on Donges, which took place in favourable weather conditions of no cloud but slight haze.

THE LAST SORTIE

Marking:
The target was marked by Oboe aircraft of P.F.F.(9 Mosquitoes) and by marker aircraft of No. 54 Base. The Oboe markers went down on time, and were assessed as 200 yards from the aiming point. A 54 base Mosquito dropped his green T.I. in a position which was assessed as 200 yards 152'. The master bomber then ordered the remaining Mosquitoes to back up the green T.I. overshooting by 200 yards.

Results:
Crews reported that a good concentration of bombs fell around the markers, and P.R.U. photographs show that a great deal of damage was done to installations and many oil tanks were totally destroyed. The oil jetty received two direct hits, and there were at least six direct hits on the railway lines supplying the site.

Control:
W/T Control was excellent and V.H.F.
R/T best results so far obtained.'

Looking at the evidence from the Station Record Book it would appear that 'G' was back over base shortly after 04.00 with the other crews, and 207 Squadron veteran Ron Winton feels it may only have been at this stage, while completing checks before landing that they realised they had a problem.

Mr. G.E. Genower, an air gunner stationed at Spilsby at the time has reason to believe that his own crew were in the circuit behind 'G'. This crew had already been assigned 'pancake' (landing) 4, but were then instructed 'pancake' 3. They queried this and were told that the aircraft preceeding them had now left the circuit. His crew accepted this and landed safely. There is no evidence to support this but it must be assumed that if it is correct, his crew, skippered by F/O N.A. Ferguson were returning from Stuttgart.

No records exist of what went on next, but we can assume the aircraft headed out to sea and that strenuous efforts were being made to jettison the bomb or bombs. Exactly what this entailed can only be guessed at as we have no evidence concerning the specific nature of the 'dangerous hang-up' reported to Spilsby when they returned.

The following description by Campbell Muirhead, a Lancaster bomb aimer in 1944, may give some idea of what was happening aboard PB 294:

'The drill was that, once the bombs had been released I told Vernon (the pilot) and asked him to close the bomb bay doors. After he'd done this I would take the Aldis lamp and shine it into the bomb bay to check that what I'd said was indeed true - that is that none of our bombs were still on board.

I'd forgotten to do this check until we were on our way back from the target, and when I slid back the panel and shone the lamp into the bay there they were, three 500 pounders, all fused, rolling about the floor of the bay. I screamed to Vernon to open the bomb bay doors, adding why. This he did and the three bombs dropped through the night onto somewhere in France.'

They'd been lucky. The oversight of checking the bay was rectified in time and the bombs were easily and quickly disposed of. Maybe the McIntosh crew had had more difficult problems? Muirhead continues as follows:

'Probably when I'd pressed the 'tit' (electrical bomb release button) these 3 bombs had come slightly adrift from their cradles, but not sufficiently enough to free them, then the movement of the 'Lanc' had gradually eased them away from the cradles and onto the bomb bay floor, where fused, they'd rolled around merely waiting for something to detonate them such as a violent corkscrew to evade a night fighter.'

The above quotations give a clear picture of what may have faced PB 294 on its return and if we consider the 'shocks' experienced on landing it becomes obvious why the crew felt that jettisoning was the only option left open to them.

The situation could indeed have been worse in that the bomb was possibly partially 'hung-up' with one end still on the cradle and the other hanging loose, a problem unlikely to be welcomed by a tired crew.

When ready to jettison Shannon would have been busy with the following procedures. First he would have tried electrical power by setting switches on his panel and employing the 'tit' as on a normal drop. If this failed then the 'bomb toggle' could have been used. This was a long piece of wire with a loop on the end, specially designed to detach bombs by hand. Finally, and by now in desperation, the crew may have had to remove the small rectangular hatch covers on the deck above the bomb bay and then worked from above attempting to physically hack the weapon free.

We do not know what happened. It could have been that the bomb was jettisoned and they then set a course for base. On the other hand it may have proved an impossibility and fuel shortage may have forced them to head westwards either to attempt a high risk landing or a ditching.

The only certainty we know is that at 05.12 the aircraft crashed into the sea.

Chapter 5 looks in more detail at the search, rescue and recovery operations which took place later that morning so there is no need to go into them here. What is of interest is that the exact position given for the accident by the search aircraft is 53.17N 00.28E, which when compared with the figures given for the jettisoning of bombs after the aborted Revigny-sur-Ornain raid makes one think. The Revigny figures, it may be recalled, were 53.16N 43.11E, and this very close similarity as to the northings seems too coincidental to be ignored, the eastings in the Revigny set of figures are simply wrong, as they place the aircraft somewhere between Moscow and Nizhniy Novgorod which doesn't seem all that likely. What, on the other hand, appears a distinct possibility is that the navigator, F/Sgt Little, had set course for, or was returning from, the same area of the North Sea they had visited only a few days previously.

CHAPTER 5: THE RESCUE ATTEMPT

The Royal Observer Corps alerted the rescue services and their information was acted on very promptly. We know from Public Record Office document AIR 29 443 that only 9 minutes after the crash, rescue and recovery operations had already been set in motion.

At 05.21 Warwick aircraft HF 947 'D' took off from Strubby airfield and proceeded towards the general vicinity of the accident. The crew of this plane were as follows:

F/O Chesher C.
F/S Jones
W/O Stewart R.
P/O Williams H.
W/O Edwards E.
W/O Donley A.

Slightly later at 05.25 a high speed launch put to sea from Grimsby tidal basin and set course for a position five miles east of Anderby Creek. This craft was one of four operated by 22 Air Sea Rescue Marine Craft Unit, but which of the four it was is not recorded.

The crew of the Warwick commenced their search but it was not until 07.55 that they were able to signal the launch to steer a course of 310', having identified the crash site by finding a large patch of oil on the surface. There was also some wreckage visible and what were believed to be three bodies in 'Mae Wests' floating in the oil patch. This sighting took place at 53.17N 00.28E.
While this was going on the Skegness Lifeboat had also been heading towards the scene, but had initially started searching at 53.10N 00.32E. The aircraft tried to contact them on V.H.F. radio but failed.

THE RESCUE ATTEMPT

It mattered little as the lifeboat soon found the correct position, possibly as a result of seeing the marine markers which the aircraft dropped. This R.N.L.I. vessel was built in 1932 by Thorneycroft and was called the Anne Allen.

R.N.L.I. Lifeboat Anne Allen

Courtesy Royal National Lifeboat Institution

The log of the Anne Allen reports their part in the operation as follows:

'On 25 July 1944, with a light wind and calm sea, Skegness Lifeboat was launched to go to a crashed Lancaster, salvaged some gear.'

Further reference to the lifeboat's involvement is given in 'A Century and a Half of the Skegness Lifeboat' by Lt.-Cdr. F.S.W. Major R.N.V.R. whose comments on the incident are as follows:

'A Lancaster bomber returning from Hamburg on July 25 1944 had a bomb jammed in the bomb rack which could not be released. The plane attempted a landing at sea close to the shore, but when it hit the water the bomb exploded, killing all the occupants and blowing the plane to pieces. The lifeboat proceeded to the last known position off Chapel St. Leonards and found some wreckage including an officer's hat and other clothing. A few days later the mangled bodies of the airmen were found on the beach.'

THE RESCUE ATTEMPT

As can be seen there are several errors in this description, but it nonetheless refers to the accident as this was the only one in the area on the day in question. If an officer's hat was indeed found it must have been that of the pilot as he was the only commissioned member of the crew.

When the launch from Grimsby eventually arrived at the crash site the crew found a partially submerged body. They tried to recover this but it sank before it could be made secure. The search continued, guided by the aircraft, eventually one other body was found and recovered. This would have been that of the pilot, who was taken back to Grimsby.

Some wreckage was also collected. This included the landing wheels, which according to one squadron veteran, found their way back to Spilsby. Maybe these were of use to the Court of Inquiry which was called. We have been told that a few days later a rear wheel 'oleo strut' was seen resting against the wall of the squadron office building. When he asked about it, our source was told that it was part of the McIntosh aircraft wreckage.

As may be remembered, the initial sightings by the Warwick mentioned three bodies being visible. It would seem likely that the other two were Bateman, the mid upper gunner, who was later washed ashore, and Little, the navigator, who was eventually found several days later.

The other four members aboard were never recovered and it can only be assumed that these men went to the bottom of the North Sea inside the aircraft and their bodies were unable to float free.

The Warwick, its work done, returned to Strubby and landed there at 09.24. The Grimsby launch continued searching until 10.00 with no success. It then returned to base arriving there at 12.00.

In closing this chapter, reproduced below is the entry from the 280 Squadron record book for 25 July 1944:

THE RESCUE ATTEMPT

'05.21 - 09.24 A S R Search Scrambled to position 53.17N 00.28E In position 53.17N 00.28E sighted wreckage of a/c. Dropped marine markers. Set course for H S L and Skegness lifeboat which was previously seen in position 53.10N 00.32E. Endeavoured to contact on VHF but failed. 'D' led H S L to position of wreckage.

Contacted H S L on Channel C and requested search for bodies which then could not be found either by H.S.L. or a/c. Carried on further search with no result. Set course for base.'

While all this was going on the coastguard contacted 207 Squadron at Spilsby to inform them of the crash. Later that day when form 540 was being typed up in the operations room, the last sentence consisted of two words. 'No Survivors'.

Already the crew had become history and would never be mentioned again in squadron paperwork. Lastly it is poignant to note at this juncture that throughout their time on the squadron several of this crew never flew over Germany, all the bombs they dropped fell in France. It makes no difference I know, but there is more than a hint of irony in the thought.

CHAPTER 6: THE AFTERMATH

This chapter has proved the hardest of all to write, as for the first time we are venturing away from research and into the area of supposition. No one knows why the aircraft crashed on that calm July morning in 1944. No one will ever know with certainty, but we feel it right to put forward the possible reasons, and then leave you, the reader, to decide for yourself what you think happened.

The facts appear to be as follows:

1.   The aircraft was in the circuit with the other five crews returning from Donges just after 04.00 hours.

2.   The pilot was aware of the problem, radioed base and let his intentions to jettison be known.

3.   He did not report any damage and seemed confident that he had enough fuel left to fly for at least another hour.

4.   He then left the circuit and was never heard from again.

5.   PB 294 was seen to crash at 05.12 by the Royal Observer Corps and did not catch fire until shortly after it hit the water.

These are all the facts we have to go on in trying to decide the cause of the fatal crash. They throw up some interesting points and also several varying possibilities of what actually happened.

We believe that there are three likely causes. These are, lack of fuel, the bomb exploding, or a catastrophic mechanical or airframe failure.

We will now look at these in turn in more detail.

Lack of Fuel:- this seems a possibility. We know that the pilot had assessed that he had at least one hour's supply left and the elapsed time between his radio message and the reporting of the crash would have used this up. It could well be that the crew had flown approximately 25 miles to the drop zone they had used on the early return from Revigny and found the bomb much harder to jettison than anticipated. They may have had to spend longer here than expected and had to go through all the procedures described in Chapter 4 before releasing the bomb, cut it too fine and crashed, or attempted a ditching on their return journey.

At this point we have conflicting evidence about what happened.

The view of F.S.W. Major outlined in chapter 5 claims ditching, but his research seems doubtful. The aircraft was not returning from Hamburg, the crash was not very close to the shore and there is contradictory evidence to suggest the aircraft wasn't 'blown to pieces' when it hit the water. If anything there is more justification to believe the main section sank more or less intact and that the four crew members who were not recovered were trapped inside the fuselage and their bodies unable to float free.

The station record book suggests that the problem arose before ditching could be attempted. The claim in this document points to the fact that suddenly the aircraft became completely uncontrollable and dived, giving the pilot no chance to ditch properly. A very different view.

In comparing the above theories several points need consideration. The station paperwork was written at the time of the incident by people closely involved. They had 'plots' from 'group' suggesting the aircraft was returning from jettisoning and they'd had no radio contact from the crew advising them of what they were intending to do. Surely they would have received further information had the crew been planning to ditch. Finally the station personnel had access to reports from the Royal Observer Corps who saw the aircraft hit the water, reports which show it did not immediately catch fire.

Using the facts outlined above it seems safe to assume that a ditching was not attempted, and therefore the crew were not, at that time at least, 'clutching at straws'. They could, of course, still have had fuel problems, either with pressure or with fuelcocks when trying to drain or switch wing tanks. Fuel remains a possible cause.

The Bomb Exploding:- we know that the crew felt it unsafe to land with the bomb on board and that they had described their problem not as a 'hang up' but as a 'dangerous hang up'. What this actually meant is not known, but it could have been that the bomb was only partially attached to the bomb carrier, or they were concerned about the time delayed fuses fitted to some of their weapons.

The two most obvious events involving the bomb are that it exploded at the jettison point while being released, or that it blew up on the way there. Both of these seem unlikely.

The aircraft was too close to the coast for it to be anywhere near the jettison area and that, if group plots are to be believed, it was on its way back. These two points alone appear to discount the first theory. The bomb did not explode at the jettison zone.

Secondly, the idea that the aircraft was still heading east towards the box. The problem here is one of time, as if it was still outbound then what had it been doing for the hour which had elapsed since it left the circuit at Spilsby? At most it would have flown forty miles which at a conservative estimate would have taken a maximum of 20 minutes. Coupled to both of the above points is the fact that the Royal Observer Corps' sighting does not in any way imply an explosion took place. In fact, if anything, this suggests that any outbreak of fire followed shortly after the accident happened.

Finally, a theory attributed to Mr. A.T. White, an air gunner on the squadron at the time, who suggests the following:

'I believe it was thought at the time that the bomb aimer dropped the hang up at too low a height.'

For this to apply we must of course assume the bomb was still on board, that the attempted jettison had been unsuccessful and lack of fuel had forced the crew to return with the 'hang up' still in the bomb bay. Possibly work to release it had continued on the return flight, a flight during which fuel concerns had led to reducing power and therefore height. It is not inconceivable that the bomb had eventually been released and that the 'splash' from it hitting the water, not an explosion, was enough to unsettle the trim and tip the aircraft forward into the sea.

Most of the above does not involve the bomb actually exploding and relies on the Royal Observer Corps' report being correct. People do make mistakes and at a distance of at least five miles the chance of this happening must be increased. As mentioned briefly above, two of the 500lb. bombs taken to Donges were fitted with six hour delay fuses, and one or both of these could have been those 'hung up'. Knowing the duration of the flight and the likelihood that the bombs were 'armed' at or shortly after the assembly point on the outward leg, then the time remaining until the accident is almost exactly six hours.

Catastrophic Failure:- this scenario is supported by the entry in the Station Record Book, which can be read above and in more detail in Chapter 4. Mr. John Hamlin concurs with this when writing in his book 'Always Prepared: The Story of 207 Squadron Royal Air Force'. He suggests the following:

'The cause of the crash will never be known, possibly the aircraft had sustained damage of which the crew were unaware'.

This is obviously a possibility as we know the aircraft had been in the area of a flak barrage which had brought down two other Lancasters involved in the operation. It may have been that the crew had experienced what they considered to be a 'near miss', which had in fact caused some damage, including the bomb 'hang up'. This could have led to a structural failure or in some way affected the controls which suddenly broke without warning causing the accident.

That concludes what we feel to be the most likely reasons for the loss of EM-G PB 294, but before we move on it is worth spending a short time on two 'long shots'.

The first scenario is that of an enemy 'intruder' aircraft being involved and shooting down EM-G as a target of opportunity. Evidence of such 'intruder' activity on the day in question would be nice to have but none can be found so again this seems most unlikely.

Secondly it is also worth considering the possibility of 'friendly fire'. It would seem from the quotation below that this could be quite a problem:

'It wasn't always the long trips that were the worst. Sometimes we got more flak near the English coast than we did over the target. That was the Royal Navy. It didn't matter what we did - shoot off the colours of the day and everything - the Navy always fired at us.'

Leonard Thompson
Flight Engineer 550 Squadron.

A thought provoking point!

All the issues so far raised in this chapter are no doubt those considered by the official Court of Inquiry. As far as can be established this took place at R.A.F. Spilsby and involved the Squadron Commander, Wing Commander J. Grey and Group Captain Harris, the Station Commander. Others may have participated but are not known.

THE AFTERMATH

Quoted below are all the comments which appear on the 'loss card' (Air ministry form 1180) and relate to the court findings. They are shown in their original context.

'0500 HRS   A/C returning from ops sortie called on R/T to say going out to sea to jettison dangerous bomb hang up. Approx 1 hour later coast guard reported a/c crashed in sea believed on fire

4:2 Possible cause lack of fuel
4:2 Lack of fuel possible cause

Bomb hung up Pilot went out to sea to jettison and on return crashed into sea and caught fire FC should before giving permission to jettison enquire the state of the fuel.

Sqn Cdr C.O.I. AOC and AOC i/c concur

4:2   A.O.C. The evidence raises a number of questions which could only be answered by the crew. Fuel shortage a possible cause AOC i/c concurs.'

N.B. 'Believed' is crossed out in the original document.

Considering the above comments it can only be regarded as an 'open verdict', but with the most probable cause being lack of fuel. It is surprising that more is not made of the bomb which was known to be stuck in the bomb bay and had been described in the radio transmission made by the crew as a 'dangerous' bomb hang up.

During the course of our research we were fortunate to come into contact with a pilot, now in his eighties, who flew Stirlings on main force operations and Lancasters with the Pathfinder Force, where he experienced 'ditching' an aircraft himself. This gentleman wishes to remain anonymous as he has, in the past, suffered abuse from people who consider the operations carried out by Bomber Command as barbaric. Having proof read our text and helped with several areas of the work we would like to include his observations.

'As you have written, the final hours leading up to the loss of the Lancaster and its crew will never be known, but I can only surmise from personal experience that the crew must have been faced with a desperate situation. i.e. a fused bomb hang up together with fuel running out. It would appear that the pilot and his crew were making every attempt to return to base safely and it must be difficult for anyone, who has not been placed in a similar situation, to imagine what must have been going on in that aircraft and particularly in the crew members minds in the run up to their tragic end.

I can only say on behalf of all surviving aircrew members and myself:

Your bravery will not be forgotten and may you rest in peace.'

In summing up, it would seem fair to say that no one who has looked into the loss of PB 294 and its crew can explain with certainty what happened. The most telling comment is that suggested by the original Court of Inquiry when they made the point that 'the evidence raises a number of questions which could only be answered by the crew.' The only real conclusion which can therefore be drawn is that it was a tragic accident, which could have been brought about by several differing sets of circumstances.

THE AFTERMATH

The Aftermath at Donges:
The following report details damage done in the target area on the nights of 23/24 and 24/25 July 1944.

It is taken from P.R.O. document AIR 51.

Confidential
30 JUL 1944
Interpretation Report No K2761
Photography by 541 Squadron on 25 JUL 1944.
Mean time of Photography: 1245 B hours.
Sortie: 106G/1645
Scale: 1/4,700 (F.L. 36")
Locality: Donges
Oil refinery and storage
(illustration 4703W/45/B)

Damage Assessment.
Cover and Quality.
All parts of the target are fully covered on photographs of excellent quality.
Period Under Review.
This report deals with all damage to the target up to 25 JUL 1944 and includes that resulting from the attacks by aircraft of Bomber Command on the nights of 23/24 and 24/25 JUL 1944.
Immediate interpretation reports Nos. K2757 and 2761 were issued on 25 and 26 JUL 1944 respectively. The former reports damage inflicted during the earlier attack whilst report K2761 covers damage accruing from the later attack.
General Statement.
As a result of these two attacks the Donges oil refinery and storage installation presents a scene of almost complete devastation. Every facility for the handling, treatment and storage of oil has been seriously affected.

THE AFTERMATH

Storage tanks of a total capacity of at least 125,000 tons have been destroyed or severely damaged. There is evidence of the destruction of large quantities of oil by fire. The boiler house, office building, workshops, water purification and refrigeration plants, packed products and filling buildings, garage and transport sheds have all been destroyed, or severely damaged, whilst the various refining and cracking installations have all suffered heavily.

The facilities for the receipt and despatch of oil by sea road and rail have all been affected and a tanker lying alongside the jetty has been badly holed and is seen lying on its side. Overhead pipelines and pump houses have been destroyed or severely damaged, thus interfering seriously with the movement of oil between the various installations.

The railway running along the northern boundary of the target area has been devastated over several hundreds of yards and traffic will be impossible until clearance and relaying of tracks has been completed.

At this stage the report becomes very difficult to read as it is badly faded. It does continue for another 3 pages and lists 45 specific sites inside the installations which have been hit with damage ranging from 'wrecked' and 'gutted' to 'slight'.

A few of the more interesting and readable examples are included below:

23)   Oil tanker (approx 450 feet): laying on side off western jetty with large rent visible amidships.

24)   Loading jetty and quay: quay and jetty both partially cut by hits. Extension jetty to west almost completely cut and pump houses and storage on quay severely damaged.

44)   St. Nazaire / Savenay Railway: two areas of destruction, each affecting over 250 yds. of tracks, four other points of damage from one or more direct hits.

45)　　Main roads serving refinery: numerous craters block roads at more than four places.

Miscellaneous damage includes:

(d)　　widespread destruction of business and residential property in the village of Donges (a defended locality) including the church.

CHAPTER 7: THE AIRFIELD TODAY

The remains of the airfield are situated approximately 3 miles to the east of the town of Spilsby and to the north and east of the village of Great Steeping, many of the dispersed sites once being in the village itself. The three runways ran as shown on the map and covered much of the rural parish of Monksthorpe. They are no longer there, neither are the vast majority of the perimeter tracks or aircraft dispersals. I was told by a local resident that they had been ripped up years ago and now form part of the foundations of the Humber Bridge.

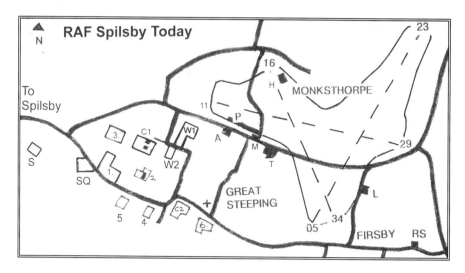

The Runways:

These were numbered 05 23, 11 29 and 16 34. The longest of these was 05 23. Nothing remains and the runway sites are now under arable farm land.

The Memorial (M):

This was built and dedicated in 2001, the official opening being in August. A small committee of the 207 Squadron Association members took on this task and their efforts speak for themselves. The memorial commemorates all those who served on 207 Squadron. It is situated

on the base of the 'fire tender' building next to the station post office, main guard room and main station entrance just to the east of the northern end of School Lane.

The Hangar (H):

You can see the sole remaining hangar from the monument when looking N.N.E. At the time of writing it has '600' painted in large letters on the side of it, and is a T2 type building. You may see a similar building to the east, near the loop dispersals mentioned later. This is a modern addition to the site.

THE AIRFIELD TODAY

Perimeter Track (P):

A single length of this remains behind the memorial and gives access to the farm. This was used to taxi aircraft round the airfield to and from the runway heads.

The Administration Site (A):

This site is situated about 300 yards west of the memorial on the opposite side of the road past the end of 'School Lane'. The site is dangerous as the buildings are in an unsafe condition. The large building with the tall chimney at the rear of the site was once the operations block where planning for raids was carried out. Nearest to the road is a large area of concrete which was the briefing room floor. It was here that aircrew gathered to be told of their next sortie. It must have been a place of high emotion. To me this simple rectangular concrete floor is the most evocative original part of the site, because of what happened there so long ago.

Between the two places mentioned above is another raised flooring area. This was the interrogation room where returning crews were debriefed after a sortie.

Signal and Operations Block

Briefing Room Floor

THE AIRFIELD TODAY

The Technical Site (T):

This is accessed by entering the 'Meadowlands' centre to the east and on the other side of the road from the memorial. In here can be seen the floor and surviving 'blast wall' of another T2 hangar. Also visible are the foundations of the motor transport section and a complete 36' by 30' temporary brick building which was originally the dinghy store. All Lancasters carried a dinghy in the starboard wing root.

This is a private site but the current owner, Mrs. Anne Smith is a very pleasant lady and could be prevailed upon to let you look around. Accommodation is available on the site as are camping and caravanning facilities but book in advance.

Loop Dispersal (L):
Situated on the eastern edge of the airfield about one mile from the technical site. This was once a loop or diamond parking area for aircraft. It's general layout can still be seen.

Other Areas (Dispersed Sites):
These are shown to the west of the map and are numbered 1 to 6, W1, W2, C1, C2. Very little remains as most of the building was hutting. The sergeants and airmens ablutions survive on site 2. This is a long low temporary brick building (Type 9). It can be seen from the road and stands in the middle of the field.

Other buildings can be seen in C1 from the road to the north of it. These are the 'standby set house,' 'officers bath house,' and 'sergeants showers,' all permanent or temporary brick structures. The letters used to label dispersed sites are as follows: 1 - 6 airmens and officers accommodation, W1 and 2 - Womens Auxiliary Air Force quarters. C1 and 2 - Communal Sites, SQ - Sick Quarters and S - Sewage.

THE AIRFIELD TODAY

The determined 'searcher' will find more, but those listed above are the most easily found remains of R.A.F. Spilsby.

Moving further afield, the Public House called 'the Bell' in Halton Holgate, between Spilsby and Great Steeping, was a favourite 'watering hole' for station personnel, a fact reflected in the sign hanging over the main door which depicts a Lancaster and refers to both 44 and 207 squadrons. Inside are several other mementoes and a squadron visitors book, which you may contribute to. The food is also very acceptable and sensibly priced.

The other popular public house was the 'Red Lion' in Great Steeping. Nowadays this is a private residence called 'Toad Hall' and is situated on the corner of the road leading towards Sandhill Farm at the western end of the village.

The church in Great Steeping, (+) on the map, contains a memorial to 207 Squadron and 44 Squadron both of which shared the airfield between October 1944 and July 1945.

Finally, if you head for Firsby and keep your eyes peeled as you drive through the village you can just make out the remains of the platform at the railway junction, (RS) on the map. This is on the left heading east next door to a large white private house which during the war was another pub called the 'The Railway Hotel'.

CHAPTER 8: OUR JOURNEY

If you've managed to wade your way through the preceding chapters you might well have wondered how the story they have told came together. Let me explain.

My mother Frances Mary Armstrong (nee Hall) was born in Boston, Lincolnshire on the 9 February 1926, and died aged 48 in Carlisle, Cumbria on the 6 May 1974. She had often talked to me, even as a small child, about the 'lads' who had stayed with her family during the war and I suppose what she said must have been interesting because I never forgot it. When she died I cleared out a lot of her possessions and decided to keep the letter, referred to in the introduction, which she had looked after for almost 30 years.

When she died my father, Joseph Armstrong, was still with us, he wasn't well, and I felt that to start delving into his late wife's past was somehow not the correct thing to do. I suppose there was an element of finding something which could have upset him, but for one reason or another the letter 'rested' undisturbed for another quarter of a century. Dad died in September 1997 and it was shortly after this that the letter again resurfaced. Goodness knows how it hadn't been lost, by now it was almost 54 years old, but there it was again and I longed to find out more.

Ruth, my wife, and I had no idea how to get started. All we had was the Christian name of Ross and an address in Newport which was many years out of date. We were interested, but if it hadn't been for the help of a close friend, David Brown of Peterborough, I suspect this whole story may well have remained untold. Dave is a keen family historian and as such was in a position to suggest a course of action to get us started. He advised us to contact the Library in Newport with the details we had, which boiled down to an address and a year, and to enquire if they could establish a surname for us. It worked. A couple of weeks after writing we received a reply and the key name of 'Shannon' was provided from electoral rolls and street directories held on records ranging from 1939 to 1946 and this proved that the family had lived at 43 Heather Road in 1944. We had a start, contacted Dave and he did the next part by finding the date Ross Shannon had died using the internet site covering allied war losses.

From this point we became more independent although it's fair to say Dave is still heavily involved with the research, particularly in the area of crew background information, where he has done a magnificent job. We established crew names, squadron and last 'op' flown from 'R.A.F. Bomber Command War Losses' by W.R. Chorley 1997, (Midland Counties Publications). We contacted the Public Records Office at Kew through a professional researcher and started to build the basic story of the crew.

By this time things were 'coming together' and by buying various books, visiting and staying on the site at Spilsby, joining 207 Squadron Association as friend members and using their archives, visiting museums and contacting the research department at R.A.F. Museum Hendon, we were getting closer to a full picture of events, but we still lacked the really detailed information we needed. We took the plunge and with Dave 'holding our hands' ventured from Carlisle to London for our first visit to the Public Records Office. After an inauspicious start which included unravelling a microfilm all over the desk, failing to master the photocopier and getting muddled by the index system we slowly got the hang of things. By late afternoon we had achieved the major breakthrough we'd hoped for and got detailed archive material which seemed so clear we could almost see the events described being enacted. We'll be back, and the next time we'll know what to do from the outset. - That could be a new project of course!

OUR JOURNEY

In search of more personal details we contacted dozens of ex-servicemen and women who had served at Spilsby during the summer of 1944 and a few more pieces of information were added. All these elderly people were so helpful and for weeks we were excitedly waiting for the postman every morning in the hope of more 'primary evidence'. We weren't disappointed.

We were also lucky in finding Graham Charters who is a leading authority on the activities of the Grimsby Air Sea Rescue Launches (ASR 22 MCU). We found a display he'd been responsible for at East Kirkby Museum, contacted him and 'hey presto' most of Chapter 5 was written for us.

Finally we tracked down Dr. Alan Grint and his mother Mrs. Alma Grint, the nephew and sister in law of the flight engineer. This contact was little more than a shot in the dark. We knew Grint had come from the Morpeth area, felt it was an uncommon name, and so searched through the telephone directory in our local public library. This produced only 3 'Grints' and our first telephone call was a winner, providing all the details included in this work. Dr. Grint had done some research himself but it had mainly concerned his family tree. It was nice to be able to reciprocate by sending both of them a copy of the finished story of their relative's crew.

Our sincere thanks go out to all who have helped, without them the McIntosh crew would have been forgotten as most young men who die in war are, once their nearest and dearest are no longer with us. I don't think it's wrong to say we are proud to have looked into their brief and bedevilled lives on active service and to have recalled a group of youngsters who paid the ultimate price of human conflict.

Research is still ongoing but we don't feel there's all that much more to uncover really and so it seems a sensible time to share our findings with others.

OUR JOURNEY

We would also like to share our feelings. These have ranged from frustration and disappointment to great 'highs' when we've found important facts. Probably the most memorable and emotional times have been when we visited Runnymede and the graves armed with flowers. It was strange, we felt we knew these boys and I freely admit to having to wipe my eyes.

We know the story told is not a happy one, but it is as honest and accurate as we can make it. Maybe you have a similar mystery you would like to unravel. If so then do it.

SORTIE COMPLETED

NOT FORGOTTEN

APPENDIX - AIRCRAFT FLOWN

During their short time operating with 207 Squadron the McIntosh crew flew several aircraft. We decided to find out what happened to these.

EM-D ND 555   Pommereval 24/25.6.44

Lancaster 111. Built by A.V. Roe at Chadderton between December 1943 and May 1944. This aircraft was eventually destroyed on the night of 6/7 November 1944 when it was tasked to attack Gravenhorst on the Dortmund Ems canal. It took off from Spilsby at 16.28 and was skippered by F/O J.E. Adams. His was an experienced crew flying their twenty ninth sortie, but all were killed and are buried in the Riechswald Forest War Cemetery. The aircraft was also something of a veteran having logged 593 hours in the air by the time it was lost.

EM-F NE 168 Mimoyeques 27/28 .6.44 St Leu D'esserent 4/5.7.44

Lancaster 111. A sister aircraft of ND 555 having been produced in the same batch by A.V. Roe at Chadderton near Manchester. Unfortunately this aircraft also failed to survive the hostilities and was lost on 6 January 1945, when tasked to bomb Houfflaize. The skipper was F/O Perez who died with five of his crew. The sole survivor was taken prisoner.

EM-P LM 535   Caen 18.7.44

Lancaster 111. Again built by A.V. Roe but this time at Yeadon near Leeds. This aircraft was a true survivor and was eventually scrapped in May 1947 at Hounslow.

EM-M LM 208   Revigny 18/19.7.44

Lancaster 1. Built in Coventry at the Whitley works of Armstrong Whitworth. This aircraft was fitted with Merlin 24 engines rather than the 38's fitted to the Lancaster 111. It was finally destroyed on the 16 November 1944 when on a 'gardening' (mine laying) operation.

F/L Montgomery and his crew were all killed when they were attacked by a night fighter near the village of Larstrup in Denmark. Reports claim the aircraft exploded in the air with great force, presumably the mines were still on board. All the crew are buried in the local cemetery near Skals.

EM-G PB 294 Donges 24/25.7.44

Lancaster 111. Built at Chadderton by A.V. Roe. Delivered new to 207 Squadron on the 10.7.44 and authorized for use on the 12.7.44. Missing 25.7.44 and struck off charge on the 27.7.44. Engines fitted were Merlin 38's and the numbers were 249433, 262545, 251072 and 244586.

What remains of this aircraft lies in the North Sea, five miles east of Anderby Creek.

LIST OF ABBREVIATIONS USED

A/C	Aircraft	O.R.B.	Operational Record Book
A.O.C.	Air Officer Commanding	O.T.U.	Operational Training Unit
A.S.R.	Air Sea Rescue	P/O	Pilot Officer
C.O.I.	Court of Inquiry	P.R.U.	Photographic Reconnaissance Unit
F.C.	Flight Control		
F/L	Flight Lieutenant	R/T	Radio Telephone
F/O	Flight Officer	T	Target
G.P.	General Purpose Bomb	T.D.	Time Delayed Fuse
H.C.U.	Heavy Conversion Unit	T.I.	Target Indicator
H.S.L.	High Speed Launch	U.S.A.A.F	United States Army Air Force
H.2.S.	Airborne Radar		
I.A.S.	`Indicated Air Speed	V.H.F.	Very High Frequency
Inst.	Instant detonation	W/T	Wireless Transmission
L.D.	Long Delayed Fuse	4J.D.	German Night Fighter Group
L.F.S.	Lancaster Finishing School		
M.C.	Medium Capacity Bomb		

ACKNOWLEDGEMENTS

Mrs. Lavinia Bonner - assistance into personal family research

Mr. David Brown - assistance into crew / general research

Mr. Glyn Brown — assistance into historical research

Mr. Graham Charters - all research in A.S.R.M.C.U.

Mr. Raymond Glynn Owen - 207 Squadron historian / archivist

Dr. Alan Grint - assistance into J. R. Grint research

Mrs. Alma Grint - assistance into J. R. Grint research

Mr. Kevin Mapley — assistance into 207 Squadron research   (Continued...)

ACKNOWLEDGEMENTS/BIBLIOGRAPHY

Mr. Ron Winton - assistance into 207 Squadron research
Staff from the following establishments:
Air Historical Branch R.A.F., Hendon R.A.F. Museum, Public Records Office, Kew, Mablethorpe Public Library, Newport Public Library, Skegness Public Library, Spilsby Public Library, Bob O'Hara - P.R.O. researcher
All 207 veterans who responded to our request for information.
Our daughter, Helen, for her help and support.
All those we've forgotten and those who encouraged us to persevere when the trail seemed to be going cold.

BIBLIOGRAPHY

Bowyer, Chaz.	Bomber Group at War	Ian Allen	1981
Charlewood, Don.	Journeys into Night	Hudson	1991
Chorley, W.R.	Bomber Command Losses of World War 11	Midland Counties	1997
Clutton Brock 0.	Massacre Over the Marne	Patrick Stephens	1994
Currie, Jack.	Lancaster Target	Goodall	1985
Freeman, Roger A.	Bases of Bomber Command Then and Now	Church House	2001
Garbutt/Golding	Lancaster	P.R.C.	1971
	Lancaster at War 5	Ian Allen	1995
Hastings, Max.	Bomber Command	MacMillan	1999
Holmes, Harry.	Avro Lancaster., The Definitive Record	Airlife	1997
Jacobs, Peter.	The Lancaster Story	Cassel	1996
Lewis, Bruce.	Aircrew	Cassel	1991
Middlebrooke/Everitt.	Bomber Command War Diaries	Penguin	1990
Muirhead, Cameron	Diary of a Bomb Aimer	Spellmount	1987
Otter, Patrick	Lincolnshire Airfields of the Second World War	Countryside	1996
Overy, Richard.	Bomber Command 1939/1945	Harper Collins	1997
Richard, Dennis.	R.A.F. Bomber Command in World War 11	Penguin	2001
Smithies, Edward.	Aces, Erks and Backroom Boys	Cassel	2002
Thompson, Walter.	Lancaster to Berlin	Goodall	1985
Yates, Harry.	Luck and a Lancaster	Goodall	1999
Hamlin, John	Always Prepared - The Story of 207 Squadron Royal Air Force	Air Britain	1999
Major, F..S.W.	A century and a half of the Skegness Lifeboat		1973

Public Record Office Documents:
AIR 14/365, AIR 14/533, AIR 14/574, AIR 14/731, AIR 14/757, AIR 27/1235, AIR 28/597, AIR 28/722, AIR 51

The authors would be pleased to hear from any reader who can add to this story. They can be contacted by writing to : Andrew & Ruth Armstrong, 37 Crosshill Drive, Morton West, Carlisle, CA2 6RS

END